MY MUSIC CONCERT

WRITTEN BY NISREEN JARDANEH
ILLUSTRATED BY DANIELLE SMITH

My Music Concert
Nisreen Jardaneh

www.nisreenjardaneh.com

Disclaimer

This book contains the ideas and opinions of its author. The intention of this book is to provide information, entertainment, helpful content, and motivation o young readers about the subjects addressed. It is published and sold with the derstanding that the author is not engaged to render any type of psychological, ical, legal, or any other kind of personal or professional advice. This children's is based on names, characters, places, and events which are products of the 's imagination. No warranties or guarantees are expressed or implied by the choice to include any of the content in this volume. The author shall not be any physical, psychological, emotional, financial, or commercial damages, but not limited to, special, incidental, consequential, or other damages. responsible for their own choices, actions, and results.

printing 2022

tions: Danielle Smith
nielle Smith

pendently Published
n Publishing Inc., Montreal, QC, Canada
xygenpublishing.com

hed

Dedication

To all music students around the world

Story of the story

Performing in a music concert can be quite nerve racking for students. That's why I always made sure to practise "how to perform" with my students before concerts so they can feel comfortable and know exactly what to expect. Many years ago, when I was working with my first autistic student, I learnt that using visuals is vital. So it came to mind why not combine visuals with storytelling about what to expect in a music concert? This story can be used as a visual guide to all students of all abilities at any time to consolidate practising and ensure a positive performance experience.

All the kids are excited.

They've been working really hard
preparing for a music concert.

It's going to be a
big day!

Do you know what a music concert is?

A music concert is a kind of a show where you play pieces on your instrument in front of people.

What instrument do you play?

What is a music piece?

A music piece is a composition that you learn to play with your teacher.

What is the name of the piece that you will perform in the concert?

Do you need to practise at home to perform in a concert?

Yes, it is important to practise your music pieces, so you can perform well and celebrate your achievement.

Do you know what happens at a music concert? Let's have a look...

You arrive at the place where the concert will be,

it could be in a music hall,

a theatre,

or

any other building.

Other music students will be there.

Also, maybe some friends and teachers.
You will meet your music teacher.

What is the name of your music teacher?

After you arrive and say

'HELLO',

you need to sit in the hall
quietly and wait for your turn to play.

Your teacher will talk to you if you need
to take breaks in the concert.

You will listen to other students play music too.
It's polite to clap at the end of each performance to show appreciation and support for each other.

The special moment is about to begin!
Your teacher will call
your name.

You will go in front of the people and present yourself by bowing to the audience..

All artists do this before they start a performance and after they finish.

You sit on the piano bench (if you play piano) or prepare your instrument. You prepare your hands and breathe. Then you start when you are ready.

TADA!!!

Your show will start!

You will play the piece you had practised in your music lessons and at home!

But what happens if you make a mistake?

DON'T WORRY!

Just keep playing and your teacher will help you if needed.

Be proud that you are trying your best.

When your turn finishes, face the audience, give a big bow and don't forget to smile.

You are a superstar !!!!
Enjoy the applause.

Then you go back to your
place and wait
quietly till the end of the
concert.
When everybody
finishes performing,
the concert will end!

You will feel VERY proud that you play a music instrument and share your love of music with others!

This is so
exciting...

LET'S GO PRACTISE!

About the Author

Nisreen Jardaneh is a music educator who believes every child should have access to music education. She has been teaching for many years and was featured as teacher of the week in Education Journal of the Middle East. She conducts workshops, presentations and seminars to promote early music education and effective use of technology in music teaching.

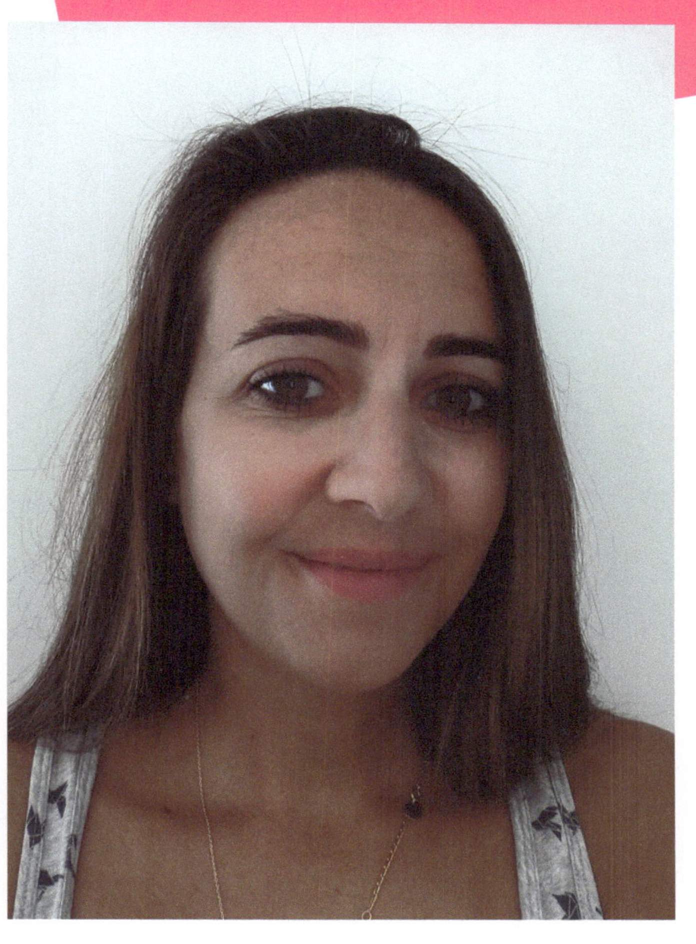

About the Illustrator

Danielle Smith is a Visual Arts educator and pastoral leader who has worked in both the U.K and currently resides in Dubai with her family. She completed her Degree at the Arts Institute and found her love of illustration whilst studying there. Danielle is passionate about the arts and believes that it should be at the forefront of today's education.

Come and find out how to make your music sparkle at

www.nisreenjardaneh.com